27

Motorbikes

Chris Oxlade

WAYLAND

First published in 2008 by Wayland
This paperback edition published in 2010 by Wayland

Copyright © Wayland 2008

Wayland
Hachette Children's Books
338 Euston Road
London NW1 3BH

Wayland Australia
Level 17/207 Kent Street
Sydney, NSW 2000

Senior Editor: Jennifer Schofield

Produced by Tall Tree Ltd
Editor: Rob Scott Colson
Designer: Darren Jordan
Consultant: Ben Russell

British Library Cataloguing in Publication Data
Oxlade, Chris
   Motorbikes. - (Machines inside out)
   1. Motorcycles - Juvenile literature
   I. Title
   629.2'275

   ISBN 13: 978 0 7502 6361 0

Printed in China

Wayland is a division of Hachette Children's Books,
an Hachette UK company.
www.hachette.co.uk

Acknowledgements
Cover Shaun Lowe/istockphoto
6–7 Makoto Ouchi, 9 Makoto Ouchi, 8 Rick Friedman/Corbis,
10 Jon Patton/istockphoto, 11t Motorcycle Cruiser Magazine,
11b Makoto Ouchi,12 Baloncici/Dreamstime.com, 13t Don
Bayley/istockphoto, 13b Worlds End Motorcycles,
14–15 Dannyphoto80/Dreamstime.com, 14 MotorcycleUSA.com,
15 calculatedrisk.ca, 16–17 Makoto Ouchi,
16 Judi Ashlock/istockphoto, 17 Mark Huntington/istockphoto,
18l Kawasaki, 18r Alexey Stiop/Dreamstime.com,
19 Jarle Eltevest, 20 Makoto Ouchi, 21b Andrew Quinlan,
21t Kerstin Klaassen/istockphoto.com, 22 Makoto Ouchi,
23b Barry Chambers/Dreamstime.com, 23t Don Splawn,
24b Mark Atkins/Dreamstime.com, 24t Honda USA,
25 Juri Bizgajmer/Dreamstime.com,
26 Dylan Sanchez/istockphoto.com, 27b Kawasaki,
27t Harry Starr/istockphoto

Note to parents and teachers
The website addresses (URLs) included in this book were valid at
the time of going to press. However, because of the nature of the
Internet, it is possible that some addresses may have changed,
or sites may have changed or closed down since publication.
While the author and Publisher regret any inconvenience this may
cause the readers, no responsibility for any such changes can be
accepted by either the author or the Publisher.

Contents

Motorbikes inside out

A motorbike is a machine built for speed. Inside are thousands of parts, from large metal tubes in the frame to tiny electronic components that control the engine. In this book, diagrams show you all the main parts of a motorbike. Here you can see the parts of a Yamaha sports bike.

Frame and bodywork

The frame is the main part of the motorbike. All the other parts are attached to it. The bodywork gives the motorbike a smooth shape.

Wheels

The wheels let the motorbike roll along the road. The tyres grip the road and help to give the rider a smooth and safe ride.

Exhaust

The exhaust carries waste gases from the engine into the air. It also stops the blast of gases from making a roaring noise.

Electrics
A motorcycle has dozens of electrical parts. These include the headlights and indicators, sensors and instruments.

Suspension
The suspension lets the wheels move up and down as the motorcycle speeds over bumps. It keeps the tyres firmly on the road.

Engine
The engine drives the motorbike along. It turns the wheels using a chain. The engine is the heaviest and most complicated part of the bike.

Motorbike frame

A motorbike has a strong frame that stretches from the handlebars back to the rider's seat and down to the engine. The frame is made from steel, aluminium or an alloy. It is made up of pieces welded together at their ends. The frame is sometimes called the chassis (say SHA-SEE).

Adding parts

The frame is like the skeleton of a motorbike. It supports all the other parts and holds them in place. Parts are bolted onto it at various attachment points. Here, parts are being added to a frame on the production line at the Harley Davidson factory in the USA.

TECH FACT

It is important that the frame does not bend, even a tiny bit. A stiff frame keeps the wheels in line with each other. This gives the motorbike good handling, which means it feels easy to ride. A bike with poor handling is hard to steer round corners, and can feel wobbly.

Frame spars

The most common frame for sports motorbikes has two pieces of metal called spars, one on each side of the motorbike. They stretch from the steering head, around the engine, and finish at the swing-arm attachment that supports the back wheel.

Cradle frames

This type of frame is called a cradle frame because it has tubes that hold up the engine from underneath. This is a strong but lightweight design, and is often used on smaller road bikes and custom bikes.

Steering head

Frame spar

Swing-arm attachment

Wheels and suspension

A motorbike's wheels let it roll smoothly along the road. The bike is supported over the wheels by the suspension. The suspension allows the wheels to move up and down as they go over bumps. This keeps the tyres on the road and also gives the rider a comfortable ride.

Suspension units

Suspension units are made up of a spring and a shock absorber. There are two units for the front wheel in the front forks. There are either one or two units attached to the rear wheel, depending on the model of motorbike.

Front fork

Forks and arms

The front forks link the handlebars and the front wheel. Each fork contains a telescopic suspension unit. The rear wheel is on a swing arm. A suspension unit controls how far it swings up and down.

Tyres

The job of the tyres is to grip the road. They let the bike accelerate, brake and corner safely. The tyres are made from rubber, strengthened with thin layers of steel. The tread pushes any water on the road out from under the tyre.

TECH FACT

A suspension unit's spring supports the weight of the motorbike above it. When the rider gets on, the springs squash a bit more with the extra weight. The shock absorber stops the spring squashing or stretching too much. It also stops the motorbike bouncing up and down after a bump.

Front fork

Swing arm

The engine turns the rear wheel, which makes the motorbike move along. Big bikes have engines with the same power as the engines in a small car. Cylinders are spaces inside the engine, about the shape and size of tin cans. Pistons fit snugly inside the cylinders, and slide up and down them.

Cylinders and pistons

Fuel burns inside the cylinders, pushing the pistons down their cylinders. Each piston has a connecting rod that pushes a crankshaft round. The crankshaft is connected to the wheels. Valves, operated by the camshaft, open to let fuel into the cylinders.

TECH FACT

The power of an engine depends on its capacity and how fast it turns. The capacity is the total space inside the cylinders. It ranges from 50 cc (cubic centimetres) in single-cylinder engines to more than 1000 cc in multiple cylinder engines. The faster an engine can turn, the more power it sends to the wheels.

Cylinders

Engine layouts

The engine in the main picture, right, has four cylinders, two on each side, arranged in a V-shape. It is known as a V-4 engine. The engine above is a V-twin, with two cylinders. This is a classic engine layout used on many American motorbikes.

Opposed engines

The photograph, right, shows one cylinder of an opposed twin engine. The two cylinders are opposite each other, one on each side of the motorbike. There are also opposed fours, sixes, and even eights. Opposed engines are also called boxer engines.

Cylinder

Camshaft

Crankshaft

Cylinder

Piston

How an engine works

As a motorbike engine runs, each cylinder follows a sequence of moves. In most motorbike engines, the sequence is the four-stroke cycle. Each piston goes in and out of its cylinder twice during the sequence. Valves open to let a mixture of fuel and air into the cylinders. Other valves open to let exhaust gases out. The fuel is ignited (set on fire) electrically by a spark plug.

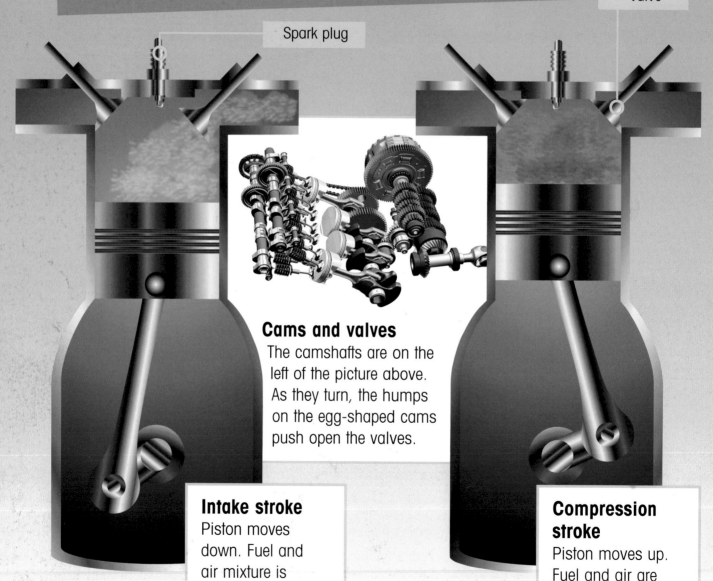

Spark plug

Valve

Cams and valves
The camshafts are on the left of the picture above. As they turn, the humps on the egg-shaped cams push open the valves.

Intake stroke
Piston moves down. Fuel and air mixture is sucked into the cylinder.

Compression stroke
Piston moves up. Fuel and air are squeezed into the top of the cylinder.

Perfect timing

This cutaway engine shows the camshafts, valves and cylinder. The camshafts are turned by a belt from the engine, and make the valves open and close at the right time during the cycle. The spark plugs work electrically. The plug produces a tiny spark that ignites the fuel.

Camshaft

Valve

Cylinder

TECH FACT

Some motorbikes have two-stroke engines. Every downstroke of the piston in a two-stroke is a power stroke. This produces more power than four-stroke engines. Two-stroke engines are also lighter as they often have no valves or camshafts. However, two-strokes are noisier and dirtier than four-strokes.

Power stroke
Fuel explodes. Piston is pushed down.

Exhaust stroke
Piston moves up. Exhaust gases are pushed out.

Fuel and exhaust

A motorcycle engine needs fuel to work. The fuel is mixed with air and burns inside the cylinders. The fuel is stored in the fuel tank and pumped along pipes to the engine. The burning fuel makes waste gases that are carried away by the exhaust system.

Exhaust parts

The exhaust system carries exhaust gases to the rear of the bike, where they go into the air. The silencer muffles blasts of exhaust gas in the exhaust pipes. This stops the motorbike making a loud noise.

The throttle

A motorbike rider twists the throttle on the right-hand handlebar to make the engine give out more power. The throttle allows more air and fuel to reach the cylinders. This makes the burning fuel push the pistons harder. So the engine speeds up, making the bike go faster.

TECH FACT

Some big sports bikes and touring machines have sophisticated engine management electronics. The electronics make the engine work very efficiently. They control the amount of fuel that goes into the cylinders, when the spark plug makes its spark, and when the valves open and close.

Right-hand handlebar

Throttle

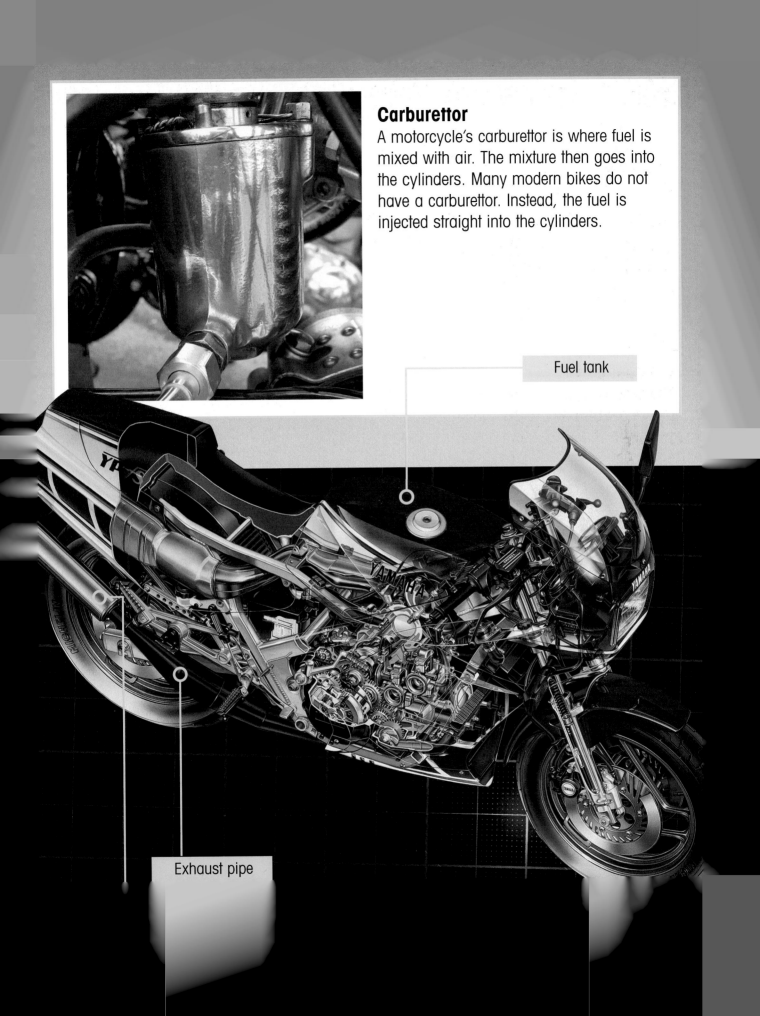

Carburettor
A motorcycle's carburettor is where fuel is mixed with air. The mixture then goes into the cylinders. Many modern bikes do not have a carburettor. Instead, the fuel is injected straight into the cylinders.

Fuel tank

Exhaust pipe

Cooling the engine

When a motorbike engine is running, it makes dozens of strokes every second, and the engine parts rub against each other at great speed. The burning fuel and rubbing generate a lot of heat. Too much heat would make the engine stop working, so the heat must be removed. This is the job of the cooling system.

Liquid cooling

Most large modern motorbike engines are cooled by water. The water flows through pipes inside the engine, carrying the heat away. The water is cooled in the radiator before it flows back to the engine.

Air cooling

Some motorbike engines are cooled by air. The cylinders have wide fins on their outsides, which get hot. As the motorbike speeds along, air cools the fins down.

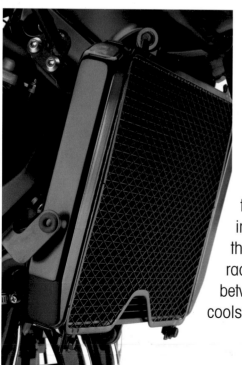

Radiator

Hot water from the engine flows into hundreds of thin pipes in the radiator. Air flowing between the pipes cools the water.

TECH FACT

Engines are filled with engine oil. The oil reduces friction by letting the engine parts move smoothly against each other. If the oil or cooling water leaks away, the engine quickly gets very hot. The parts expand and jam against each other, and the engine seizes up.

Radiator

Cooling water pipe

Water pump

Transmission

A motorbike's transmission connects the engine to the rear wheel. It is made up of the clutch, the gearbox and the chain. The transmission lets the rider start and stop the motorbike, and ride at different speeds without the engine running too slowly or too quickly.

Chain

Rear sprocket

Gearbox

Chain drive

There are toothed wheels called sprockets on the gearbox and the rear wheel. They are linked by a chain so that the gearbox can turn the wheel. A few touring bikes have a shaft drive instead of chain drive.

Sprocket

Chain

Gears and clutch

Gears change how fast the engine turns the rear wheel. Low gears are used for starting off or riding slowly, high gears for fast riding. The clutch disconnects the gearbox from the engine before changing gear.

TECH FACT

Motorcycles have sequential gears. The rider lifts the gear-change pedal to change up a gear, and presses down to change down a gear. The rider must change gear in order, or sequence. This is different from a car, where the driver can change from any gear to any other gear by using the gear lever.

The gearbox

The gearbox contains cogs on two shafts. One shaft is turned by the engine and the other turns the rear wheel (via the chain). When the rider selects a gear, a cog on one shaft interlocks with a cog on the other shaft.

Main shaft turned by engine

Shaft to rear wheel

Steering and brakes

A motorbike rider steers by pushing and pulling on the handlebars. This turns the front forks, which turn the front wheel. The rider also has to lean over on corners. Brakes slow down a motorcycle. Each wheel has a type of brake called a disc brake.

Brake lever

Headstock

Handlebar

Brake pedal

Brake disc

The headstock

The front forks are joined to the motorbike frame at the headstock. The headstock stops the forks from wobbling but lets them twist from side to side. This is very important for controlling the bike, especially at high speeds.

Headstock

Discs and pads

There is a metal disc attached to each wheel. A calliper unit is attached to the front forks and to the rear swing arm. This contains two brake pads. When the rider applies the brakes, the pads squeeze the disc, which slows the wheel.

Brake controls

The front brake is applied by a lever on the right-hand handlebar, and the rear brake is applied by the right foot pedal. On small bikes the brakes are operated by cables. Larger bikes use fluid in pipes.

Brake lever

TECH FACT

Some heavy touring bikes have a system called anti-lock braking (ABS). If the rider applies the brakes too hard, the wheels can stop turning suddenly. The ABS detects this and releases the brakes slightly. This stops the bike from skidding, and brings it to a stop quickly and safely.

Safety and comfort

Motorbikes have several features to make their riders as safe as possible. For example, some large bikes have anti-lock brakes (see page 23), and bikes can be fitted with sidebars to protect the rider's legs if the bike topples over. Riders' clothing and other equipment also help to keep them safe and comfortable.

Protective clothes

Motorcycling clothing is designed to protect riders from the wind and rain, and from bumps and scrapes if they fall off their bikes. Jackets and trousers are made from leather or artificial fabrics. There is extra padding at the knees, elbows and shoulders. The helmet protects the head and is the most important piece of safety equipment.

Airbags

The Honda Gold Wing is the only motorbike to have an airbag for the rider. There are sensors in the front forks which can tell if the front wheel hits something at high speed. The airbag then automatically inflates to stop the rider flying over the handlebars.

Taking passengers

Many bikes have a seat large enough for two people. The passenger is said to be riding pillion. He or she holds onto a bar behind the seat, and must keep very still around corners so that the bike handles smoothly.

TECH FACT

Modern motorcycle helmets have a strong plastic outer shell. Inside the shell there is a thick layer of expanded polystyrene that soaks up the energy of a collision. All makes of helmet are tested to make sure that they will protect a rider properly.

Helmet

Visor

Chin guard

Leather jacket

Leather trousers

Protective gloves

Padded boots

Quad bikes

A quad bike is an off-road vehicle based on a motorbike. It is a cross between a bike and a small car. The word quad means 'four', and quad bikes have four wheels. Most quad bikes are made by motorbike manufacturers, such as Honda, Yamaha and Kawasaki. The proper name for a quad bike is an all-terrain vehicle (ATV for short).

Bike-like features

Quad bikes have motorbike engines. The rider sits astride the bike, with one leg on each side. The controls are similar to the controls on a motorbike. The rider steers with handlebars, which turn the front wheels.

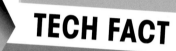

TECH FACT

Quad bikes have engines very similar to motorbike engines. They are either four-stroke or two-stroke, and range in capacity from 50 cc to 1000 cc. Sports quads have large two-stroke engines for maximum power. Most utility quads have four-wheel drive, and most sports quads have two-wheel drive.

Quad-bike suspension

Each wheel on a quad bike has its own suspension unit, with a spring and shock absorber. Here the suspension units are painted yellow.

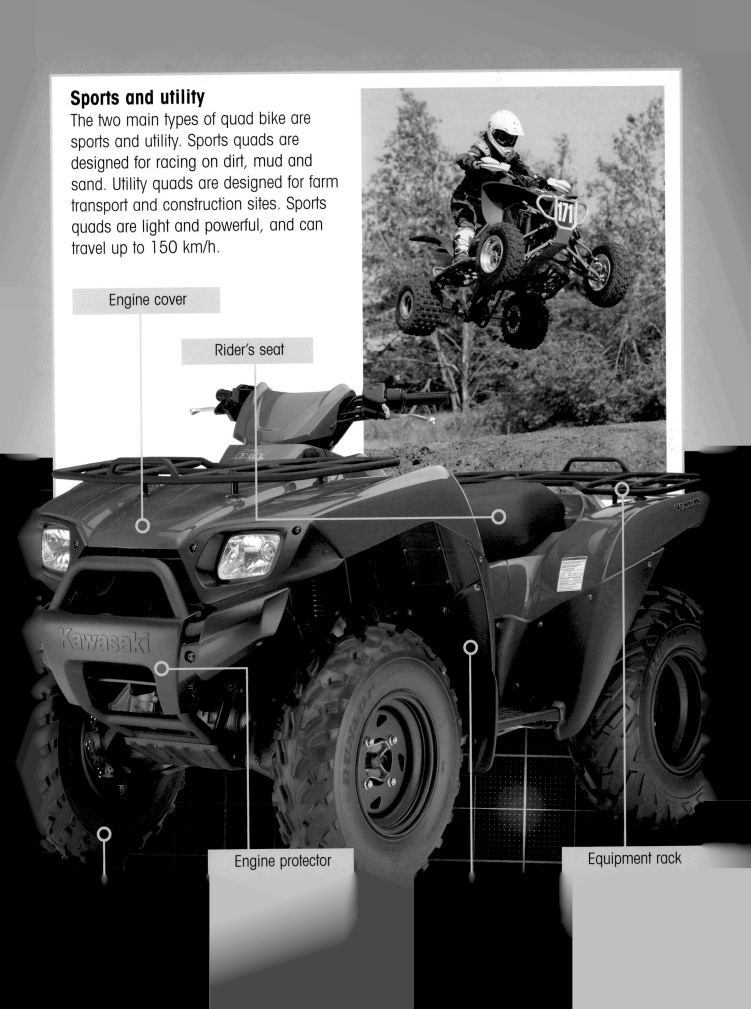

Sports and utility

The two main types of quad bike are sports and utility. Sports quads are designed for racing on dirt, mud and sand. Utility quads are designed for farm transport and construction sites. Sports quads are light and powerful, and can travel up to 150 km/h.

Engine cover

Rider's seat

Engine protector

Equipment rack

Glossary

Accelerate
To speed up.

Alloy
A material made from two metals
or a metal mixed with another
material.

Cog
A wheel with teeth around
its edge.

Component
An object that is part of a larger,
more complex machine.

Cylinder
A space inside an engine where
fuel burns.

Exhaust
The parts of a motorbike that carry
waste gases away from the engine.

Four-stroke
An engine in which there is a power
stroke on every other downstroke of
the pistons.

Frame
The main part of a motorbike, which
keeps the bike rigid and supports all
the other parts.

Hydraulic
Describes a machine that has parts
moved by liquid pumped along pipes.

Piston
Part of an engine that slides up and
down a cylinder.

Sensor
A device that detects things, such
as the temperature in an engine or
when a fuel tank is empty.

Shock absorber
Part of the suspension that stops
the spring getting too squashed or
stretched.

Skid
When a motorbike slides along the
road without one or both of the wheels
turning. A skid happens when the tyres
lose their grip on the road.

Suspension
Part of a motorbike that lets the wheels
move up and down as the motorbike
goes over bumps.

Suspension unit
Part of a motorbike's suspension,
made up of a spring and a
shock absorber.

Swing arm
The part of a motorbike suspension that connects the rear wheel to the frame. The swing arm lets the rear wheel move up and down.

Two-stroke
An engine in which there is a power stroke on every downstroke of the pistons.

Valve
Part of an engine that opens temporarily to let fuel into a cylinder or exhaust gases out of a cylinder.

Welding
A way of joining two pieces of metal together by heating them up until they melt and pressing them together so that they form a strong joint.

Further reading

The World's Greatest Motorbikes
Ian Graham (Raintree, 2005)

Extreme Machines: Motorbikes
Chris Oxlade (Watts, 2006)

Top Trumps ultimate motorbikes
Roland Brown
(JH Haynes and Co, 2006)

Useful websites

auto.howstuffworks.com/motorcycle
Guide to how motorbikes work.

auto.howstuffworks.com/engine1
Animation of the four-stroke engine cycle.

www.keveney.com/twostroke.html
Animation of the two-stroke engine cycle.

powersports.honda.com/motorcycles
Official site of Honda motorcycles.

www.bmw-motorrad.com/com/index
Official site of BMW motorcycles.

Index